the first summer study book for viola

by cassia harvey

CHP187

©2007 by C. Harvey Publications All Rights Reserved.
www.charveypublications.com - print books
www.learnstrings.com - PDF downloadable books
www.harveystringarrangements.com - chamber music

Viola Note Chart

3. What Do You Do With a Drunken Sailor?

4. Drunken Sailor String Crossing

©2007 C. Harvey Publications All Rights Reserved.

5. Fiddle Tune

6. Rossini's William Tell

9. Oh Susannah

Foster/arr. Harvey

10. Susannah's Exercise

©2007 C. Harvey Publications All Rights Reserved.

11. Mountain Exercise

12. She'll Be Comin' Round the Mountain

©2007 C. Harvey Publications All Rights Reserved.

13. Sleep Exercise

14. Are You Sleeping?

15. Sleeping Yet?

©2007 C. Harvey Publications All Rights Reserved.

16. Finger Trainer

17. Michael, Row the Boat Ashore

18. Find the Hidden Songs

©2007 C. Harvey Publications All Rights Reserved.

19. Bugler's Exercise

20. Reveille Bugle Call

21. Bugler's Next Exercise

22. Assembly Bugle Call

22. Taps Bugle Call

Remember: A dotted half note gets 3 counts.

©2007 C. Harvey Publications All Rights Reserved.

23. Finger Running

24. Swallowtail Jig

©2007 C. Harvey Publications All Rights Reserved.

25. Playing on G and D

26. Buffalo Gals

27. Blow the Man Down

28. Arpeggios

29. On Top of Old Smoky

32. This Old Man

33. Double Trouble

©2007 C. Harvey Publications All Rights Reserved.

34. String Crossing

35. Simple Gifts

©2007 C. Harvey Publications All Rights Reserved.

36. Using the 4th Finger

37. Battle Cry of Freedom

Root/arr. Harvey

©2007 C. Harvey Publications All Rights Reserved.

40. Home on the Range

Kelley/arr. Harvey

41. Hail to the Chief

Sanderson/arr. Harvey

42. Yankee Doodle

©2007 C. Harvey Publications All Rights Reserved.

available from **www.charveypublications.com**: CHP304

Beginning Fiddle Duets for Two Violas

Cripple Creek

Trad., arr. Myanna Harvey

©2016 C. Harvey Publications All Rights Reserved.

www.ingramcontent.com/pod-product-compliance
Lightning Source LLC
Chambersburg PA
CBHW051432070526
44584CB00023B/3692